"This book is for ~~...~~
and who finally see that ~~...~~
Liz understands the heart of the struggling ~~...~~
understands where true hope is found. *The End of Me* points moms to the gospel of Jesus Christ, where grace is received, identity is restored, and true obedience begins."

EMILY JENSEN, Co-author, *Risen Motherhood: Gospel Hope for Everyday Moments;* Co-founder, Risen Motherhood ministry

"Two things ring true for most moms. One is that we often enter into motherhood with confident excitement and hopeful expectations. The second is that reality always hits. Although motherhood is a blessing and a gift, sooner or later challenges, stresses, and the unexpected begin to shake our confidence and bring us to the end of ourselves. And we wonder, 'Am I the only one?' For that reason, I'm thankful that Liz Wann has written *The End of Me* for every mom who feels they fall short of the mom that they desire to be. With a fresh and honest perspective, Liz not only acknowledges the realities of motherhood, but she also shows us how the weakness and insecurities we face may be the very things that lead us to a strength beyond ourselves—a strength that comes only through Jesus."

SARAH WALTON, Author, *Hope When It Hurts* and *Together Through the Storms*

"We all learn by experience that life's most rewarding things are often also life's most difficult things. Parenting is certainly no exception, and part of what makes it so tough is the sense of failure that so often accompanies it. If you're a parent, and specifically a mother, who is aware of your failings, aware of your shortcomings, aware that you aren't exactly the mother you thought you'd be, then this book is for you. Its promise is not that it will make mothering easy, but that it will point you to the hope and confidence God offers you through the gospel of Jesus Christ."

TIM CHALLIES, challies.com

"A breath of fresh air, *The End of Me* gives a realistic, Christ-centred view of motherhood, with all of its ups and downs. I am confident that Liz's honesty about her own struggles will help women not just to survive but to grow closer to Christ through the joyful privilege of parenting a child."

LINDA ALLCOCK, Author, *Head, Heart, Hands* and *Deeper Still*

"Motherhood is the hardest job I've ever had. It's revealed the depths of my sin, my profound weakness, and my great need for Christ. That's why I was so encouraged by Liz Wann's book, *The End of Me*. This book is gospel-centered encouragement for all moms who struggle with the hard days of motherhood. Liz directs our eyes to see how Christ is formed in us as we die to ourselves and rise to life in him."

CHRISTINA FOX, Counselor; Speaker; Author, *Idols of a Mother's Heart* and *Sufficient Hope: Gospel Meditations and Prayers for Moms*

"We all enter motherhood with idealistic hopes and dreams. But the reality of sleepless nights, sick children, and temper tantrums can lead us to despair. Liz Wann's honest look at motherhood will encourage you to find resurrection hope and joy through the very trials that bring us to the end of ourselves."

STACY REAOCH, Author, *Wilderness Wanderings*; regular blogger at Desiring God, TGC, Revive Our Hearts

Liz Wann

The End of Me

thegoodbook
COMPANY

*To my husband, Josh, because I couldn't have done
any of this without your help and support.*

*To my beautiful children, Simon, Eli, and Chloe,
for teaching me how to live and love.*

The End of Me
© Liz Wann, 2021

Published by:
The Good Book Company

thegoodbook.com | thegoodbook.co.uk
thegoodbook.com.au | thegoodbook.co.nz | thegoodbook.co.in

ISBN: 9781784985752 | Printed in the UK

Design by André Parker

Contents

Foreword

by Blair Linne

Before I had my first child, I remember several people telling me, "Blair, you're going to be a great mother." They said this because they knew I'd been a nanny for years and that I loved children. So imagine my shock when I learned that not only was labor hard, but life after delivery wasn't any easier! In those first weeks and months, I faced the challenge of nursing, watched my husband drive off for meetings while I felt stuck at home with the baby blues, and cluster-fed my infant while covered in spit-up. It was a challenge. When I needed a shower, my baby would cry. When he was hungry, he would cry. When he was overly tired, he would cry. Eventually, I started to cry too.

Those days were filled with tears, fears, and questions for God. I wondered why the blessing of a child felt like a trial. I wondered if I was just profoundly sinful to feel this way. I look back on those days and I can see how the Lord was seeking to work his gospel in me through it all. He wanted me to know that he was bottling every one of my tears. And he wanted me to reach the end of myself so that I could be a *reflector*. Reflectors are those small squares on the back of bikes that catch light and alert onlookers so that they can avoid a crash. I realized that God wanted me, in a similar way, to reflect his light to my children so that they might be warned and awakened to God's light—and, Lord willing, be kept from harm on life's highway.

The good works that God has called us to as mothers cannot be accomplished apart from the good news of Christ. Yet we are often tempted to believe that the more we do in our own strength, the better mothers we will be. In this book, Liz reminds us that instead of placing our confidence in what *we* do, we must redirect our attention toward what our Savior has done. Only then can we do the good works he desires to do through us.

Liz was raised in a Christian home; I was not. She was raised by both parents; I was raised in a single-parent home. We grew up on opposite coasts—she's from Florida, and I'm from California. But despite these different experiences growing up, today we share similar struggles as mothers. We both currently live in Philadelphia, we were married in the same year, and we each have three precious children—two boys and a girl. Even if you don't share as much in common as Liz and I do, I think that most mothers can relate to the common struggle and challenge of motherhood. No matter what your background is, where you live, or how many children you have, motherhood can be hard.

The temptation to find our identity in what we do as mothers—rather than resting in the work that Jesus accomplished on our behalf—is a common one. His death and resurrection have eternally transformed our position before God, and that should change how we live. We should be driven by grace, yet we can easily be tempted toward the pursuit of perfectionism. We want things to work out just right in our marriage and with our children so that we can boast in our accomplishments, even if just a little. It's this secret pride that the Lord continues to crucify so that our confidence is not in anything but him. Perfectionism is not the goal of motherhood—*faith* is.

In order to purify our faith and make us more Christ-like, God uses trials and suffering. It is rare these days to hear this message of death to self. Instead, we are surrounded by the world, the flesh, and the devil telling us to live for ourselves, not to die to ourselves. That's why I'm so thankful for Liz's book, which provides practical wisdom rooted in Scripture on how to deny ourselves each day so that we may truly live out the gospel in the context of motherhood.

We die to ourselves and live unto God when we pick up LEGOs, train little hearts, make meals, repeat Scriptures, redirect tantrums, fold endless loads of laundry, and keep giving to others out of the abundant reserve that only comes through the Spirit. Our righteousness is secured through Jesus' perfect life, death, and resurrection, not through being perfect at motherhood—and that truth, when daily remembered and embraced, is freeing.

May God be glorified in our daily crucifixions as we do the holy work of mothering through the strength of our generous Father.

Blair Linne, January 2021

Introduction:
Mama, You Got This?

During my first few years as a mom, I began to see that I wasn't who I thought I was.

I wasn't as patient as I thought.

I expressed anger I didn't know I was capable of.

I didn't have the capacity I thought I had.

I wasn't able to be *that* mom: the one who could get it all done and never feel tired or take time for herself.

I was not the kind of mom who could say, "I got this." All too often, in fact, I hadn't "got this" at all.

As a young mom, I had devoured books on motherhood. And while they were all encouraging and gospel-centered, they seemed to neglect some of what I was experiencing. They didn't really talk about motherhood's darkest struggles—topics like postpartum depression or birth trauma. Though the books I read cast a high vision of hope and calling, they only felt relatable on a surface level. The conversations I was having with other moms were the same—most women keep silent about these deeply challenging aspects of motherhood. The truth is, none of us have "got this"—not on our own.

On a superficial level, I kept up appearances (most of the time). But beneath the surface, I was struggling. Motherhood felt harder and more sacrificial than I'd expected from anything I had read or heard. Motherhood felt as if I was coming to the end of me. Some days I wasn't quite sure who I was anymore, or what had happened to the woman who first held that positive pregnancy test—and that was scary.

And then I realized: this is how it is, and that's ok. And more than that—this is where I meet Jesus.

What I eventually figured out was that all those daily "deaths" of motherhood were producing the life of Christ in me. I had to come to the end of myself and of the self-sufficient idea that I was able to do it all. When I submitted to the truth that I wasn't enough, that I couldn't do it all, and that I was limited, that's when I felt free to embrace motherhood's daily struggles as a means of growth in godliness. Coming to the end of who I was, and seeing what motherhood was stripping me of, was a good thing because it drove me to Christ and to the power that he supplies in every failure and weakness of motherhood.

God works in and through our weaknesses. He is in the business of making all things new. It's a process of turning back the decay of the fall and laying new seed for harvest. He's killing the old—purging, refining—to bring back life. The Lord will keep doing this in us until we see him face to face, when he'll do it finally once and for all with the whole of creation.

Jesus put it this way: "Truly, truly, I say to you, unless a grain of wheat falls into the earth and dies, it remains alone; but if it dies, it bears much fruit" (John 12 v 24). Jesus was speaking of his own crucifixion and resurrection (v 23), *and* about the life his followers would experience (v 25). This dying and burying was a one-time act for our salvation, but it's also a continual act for the Christian. We continue to put to death that which is death in us (sin), and as we do that, God promises us new life in him.

The struggles and sacrifices of motherhood can lead to life. We're taking up our "cross", as Jesus took up his, because of the joy set before us. We're laying down the expectations we had of motherhood; we're admitting our weakness and bringing it to God as he uses it to show us more of his power and strength.

Everyone's experience of motherhood is different. But I've never yet met a mom who didn't, if she was being honest, find it hard—and, at times, *too* hard. I've never yet met a Christian mom who didn't feel she was failing and flailing. So if you're in that place right now, well, welcome to motherhood! And welcome to this book. I wrote this book for you, and I hope that as you read, you'll find that those moments we all tend to try to avoid—when we come to the end of ourselves—are actually moments to press into, to find hope in, and to seek Jesus through. This book won't make mothering easier, but it will offer you life in the moments and places when and where it feels as if you just gave yours up.

More often than not, I can't say to myself, "Mama, you got this!" And that's ok—because I know someone who has got this: someone who knew what it meant to be weary and tired, someone who needed some "me time," someone who sacrificed himself (even his own body) for others, and someone who died and rose again.

You've got this, mama, because you've got *Jesus*.

CHAPTER 1

Jesus Meets Us in the Hard Moments

When I was pregnant with my first child, I had a carefully crafted birth plan, and that plan did *not* involve an induction. I was supposed to do most of my labor at home, but instead all of my labor was spent in a hospital room for twenty-four hours. I was trying my best to keep everything natural when it came to induction and avoiding a c-section, but the pressure was on us with doctors and nurses who had their own time schedule. My labor crept on, and my fears heightened. Maybe I'll need to have a c-section? Will this baby ever come? His heart rate was an issue from the beginning, so there was always that lingering fear in my mind too. Would my baby be ok? I cried from all the fear, stress, and weariness. I was physically, mentally, and emotionally exhausted.

Most stories of childbirth I'd heard before sounded magical. "The baby comes out, and the instant love you feel is amazing," other moms had told me. "There's nothing else in the world like it." The tears of joy, the warmth of emotion, and the instant bond of love that seemed normal from other birth stories raised my expectations. But when I had my first son, I didn't experience any of those things. My long labor was followed by a long and hard delivery. I pushed for an hour and a half. He was coming out face up, which made it more difficult. My mind eventually went blank. I don't remember much—some words and images are blurs in my brain. When my son came out and my doctor told me how long it had been, I was shocked. My mind had lost its sense of time, and my body had taken over.

I didn't feel that initial warm mother-and-baby bond. I held my son for a few seconds, and then he was wheeled to the NICU so that they could monitor some issues with his lungs. I remember feeling relieved that he was taken away for a little while. But mostly my feelings were numb; my body and brain were in shock. This was not the warm birth experience I'd been expecting.

When we got home, my son would be up all night crying; I would be crying too. He wanted to be near me all the time. When evening crept in, I would dread the coming hours. He always knew when I put him down and would cry for me to hold him again. Even after nursing, he still wouldn't calm down and go to sleep for my husband or me. And the nursing was an issue that wore me down too. Breastfeeding had been part of my plan, but no one had told me how painful or how hard it could be. It was another element that was talked about as beautiful and natural, but for me it was neither of those things. It took weeks (and I almost gave up) until breastfeeding was good for both of us.

I was so stressed out: trying to get my son on a schedule, doing all I could to get him to sleep through the night and not let him into my bed, and just trying to do all the things I thought I should do. My own body turned against me as well. As my changing hormones raged inside me, I felt lonely all the time and cried a lot for no reason. All these feelings took me by surprise. This was not my plan. Surely this could not be motherhood. Or at least not the motherhood of my dreams.

WALKING IN THE TENSION

I now know that motherhood is a tension between sorrow and joy; that a long painful labor is normal for many; and that some moms experience a birth that is far more traumatic than mine. I had plans and dreams for how it would be as a first-time mom—even when it came to labor and deliver—dreams that turned out to be unrealistic. Unexpected events and hardships, a difficult birth, and the baby blues all collapsed my ideals. I loved my baby, but I didn't have that immediate connection that I later I formed with my other two. Because of everything that happened, it took me many weeks to bond with him. I was drawn to him and yet felt distant from him. It was not what I had expected motherhood to be like. In my mind it was supposed to be a nurturing and warm experience, but my nurturing felt more robotic than warm.

I was surprised at my lack of feelings and by how hard motherhood was. At the time I didn't know this period would be over soon; I just felt knocked down. And yet I discovered something unexpected and very precious. The Lord showed me that this period of motherhood was an opportunity. It was a painful stripping of myself to open up paths yet unknown in following Jesus. There was a light at the end of the temporary tunnel of darkness.

In Isaiah 30 we're told that

> though the Lord give you the bread of adversity and the water of affliction, yet your Teacher will not hide himself anymore, but your eyes shall see your Teacher. And your ears shall hear a word behind you, saying, "This is the way, walk in it," when you turn to the right or when you turn to the left.
>
> Isaiah 30 v 20-21

I knew this was the way I was meant to take. The Lord was beckoning me to walk the straight and narrow way and to not turn off the path, though it was dark and unexpected. Jesus had walked a tunnel of darkness too, but he kept his eyes on the light ahead of him—the joy that comes in the morning: the joy of resurrection (Hebrews 12 v 2). Instead of just seeing my struggles as hardship, I wondered how God would redeem these unexpected challenges and "raise me up" with him?

THE PERFECT IDEAL

Many moms I talk to have similar experiences. One of my friends, Lara d'Entremont, recently wrote about her expectations of motherhood:

I had plans for what my life would look like when my baby came. When we first brought him home, I spent one of his naps creating an hour-by-hour schedule for our weeks. Mondays look like this, and on Tuesdays I will do this, etc. Each day was blocked out with writing, reading, cleaning, studying, and space for the frequent nursing and naps. I can hear the well-seasoned mothers laughing—I quickly learned that babies don't naturally conform to schedules. Levi didn't wake up and go to sleep based on what I wrote in my agenda. I struggled to find what I deemed to be adequate time in Scripture with the tumbling of my "perfect" schedule.

Like Lara, all moms can relate to carefully laid plans gone awry. We are left scrambling to pick up the broken pieces of our ideal and to work out how to rearrange them and put them back together: whether it's a daily schedule for yourself and your children, figuring out how to balance work and family, health problems, a medical diagnosis, or even the grief of miscarriage and infertility. Maybe we also didn't realize the toll a new baby would have on our marriage. Growing a family can bring new things to light and bring tension in our relationships.

Another friend of mine, Laura Lundgren, said she had a perfect ideal in her head of what kind of mother she would be, but as motherhood altered her expectations, she realized that her focus needed to be more on *repentance* than perfection. I have found that perspective so helpful as I look at my own experiences.

All types of women come to the table of motherhood with an ideal in mind, and when we, or our experiences or feelings, fall short, we feel guilty. But God allows these unplanned feelings and experiences to come into your life to remind you of his grace. To bring you back to him. Wonderfully, he wants to exchange your guilt for his grace. He wants you to rely on him more.

CHRIST'S POWER RESTS ON WEAK MOTHERS

Once I accepted that I couldn't always force this little human to do what I wanted, I relaxed, became more flexible, and enjoyed my time with my baby. To my surprise, I found that I was being molded and shaped more than he was.

I remember using the late nights and early mornings as an opportunity to cry out to God. I would be rocking my son to sleep, while playing hymns and trying to read my Bible on my phone. Many times as a first-time mom I felt so depleted and weary. I just felt needy. I started to think, "Maybe this is the redemption God has planned for me? Maybe these feelings and unexpected hardships are part of his plan." Sitting in that rocking chair at four in the morning, with my son in my arms and whispering prayers of desperation to God, turned out to be his perfect place for me.

The place of neediness and desperation is one we all try to avoid. It feels awkward and uncomfortable. And it's also very humbling. But God lets us walk through these dark tunnels of unexpected challenges and feelings to remind us of who *we* are and who *he* is. He is unchanging and unshakable. We are weak and fallen with wavering hormones and shakable plans. He gives grace to the one who knows this and accepts it. He gives grace to the humble (James 4 v 6). This is the essence of humility: having a right understanding of ourselves in relation to God.

And the Lord knows that this is the path of redemption: the path that leads us to be more like him.

> *For this light momentary affliction is preparing for*
> *us an eternal weight of glory beyond all comparison.*
> *2 Corinthians 4 v 17*

He is shaping us to be more like Jesus (Romans 8 v 29). This is how God views our unexpected feelings and hardships. They are in-built elements of humanity; they are not necessarily obstacles or drawbacks, as we would view them, but they can lead to advances in the kingdom of God; they are intended to draw us deeper into our relationship with Christ. What feels like a drawback can, in fact, bring about an advance.

The Lord is creating opportunities to shower more grace on you, to draw you closer to him as you rely on him to give you strength. Just as your own baby expects you to come to them when they cry, so God comes to you when you cry to him as a weak and helpless babe.

JESUS KNOWS

In the magazine *Common Place Quarterly*, April Brover says this:

> *We are created to be in communion with our*
> *Creator. It is righteous for us to need him and good*

> *for us to feel desperate when our tanks are running*
> *low ... God delights in hearing us plead with him in*
> *prayer for his sustaining grace; his tank never runs*
> *low. He is always near and full to the brim with all*
> *that we lack, whether it be patience, grace, vision or*
> *love. It is his fullness that enables and renews us.*
>
> *p 32*

Jesus knows what it's like to have his tank run low. He has been human like us. He has known what it's like to feel need and to be desperate. He wrestled with strong emotions. So, when we cry to our God in heaven to help us in our time of need, we don't have to fear that he won't understand. "He knows our frame" (Psalm 103 v 14): he knows how we are made. He knows because he's our Maker, but he also knows because he experienced it. He walked this earth as a human, so we could come to him when we are weak. He made himself weak to the point of death, so we could know his divine strength.

The apostle Paul had some type of chronic weakness of which we don't know the details, and he said this:

> *But [the Lord] said to me, "My grace is sufficient*
> *for you, for my power is made perfect in weakness."*
> *Therefore I will boast all the more gladly of my*
> *weaknesses, so that the power of Christ may rest*
> *upon me.*
>
> *2 Corinthians 12 v 9*

Jesus left us with the Spirit as our helper (John 14 v 16-17). It is the Holy Spirit who works this strength in us. When we know and accept our weakness as moms and use it as an opportunity to cry out to God for help, the Spirit rushes in with the power made available to us by the life, death, and resurrection of Christ himself.

The biblical call of a mother is to lead her children to Christ: to train them in the ways of his word and to rely on his Spirit, and to equip them in their faith. Christ's power is guaranteed to equip every mother committed to this call, for Christ's power rests on weak mothers. This is where his strength is clearly seen. And it is so much better than any human strength we try to muster up on our own.

So, we don't need to hide our weaknesses—to hide the unexpected feelings or deny our unexpected challenges—but we can boast in them (2 Corinthians 12 v 9) as we offer them to Christ in exchange for his power. Our ideal dream for motherhood might not have panned out, but that was the plan all along: the plan of redemption sovereignly orchestrated by God himself to give us strength in our weakness; to meet us in our neediness; to give us the grace we need so much more than our well-contrived plans.

RUN TO HIM

It's good for moms to be well prepared. There is nothing wrong with making plans. We all have different ideals and ideas for ourselves and our children, but sometimes reality comes crashing in to take their place. And yet, the unexpected was God's plan all along: a plan to draw us to himself, to get us to rely on his strength in our weakness. This is his way of redeeming our unexpected hardships. And when we come to him, he gives us what we need: more grace. So, run to him with the unexpected feelings and hardships of motherhood. He will meet you in your time of need (Hebrews 4 v 16).

FOR YOUR HEART AND LIFE

(At the end of each chapter I've included a "For Your Heart and Life" suggestion. These are simple action points that will help you to apply what you've been reading to your own life and heart.)

Look at a picture from when you were pregnant. Think about what your expectations were for motherhood and reflect on the ways that motherhood has not been what you thought it was going to be. Then think about how God might be using these unexpected outcomes to your benefit.

Dear Father,

You hold all circumstances in your hands: the ones I plan for and the ones I don't. Please help me to trust that you are in control over all the hardships and feelings I will encounter in motherhood. Help me to humble myself in my weakness and come to you for strength. Let me see these challenges as an opportunity to draw closer to you and as a reason to run to you for more grace. You are with me, and you are here for me. Remind me that my neediness is part of your plan of redemption for me as you change me to the image of your Son, to become more like him in his character. Thank you for choosing what's best for me in spite of what I thought was best.

In Jesus' name, Amen

Journaling Space

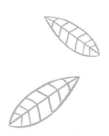

CHAPTER 2

Finding Glory in the Mundane

Since becoming a mom, I always feel speechless when people ask me how my week was. I give them a blank stare while I try to think about it. I'm always grasping for something that happened that was a big deal, or an event, or something with some element of excitement to it. Sometimes I do have something exciting to share (or at least my mommy-mundane version of exciting—got a toddler potty-trained, anyone?), but most of the time I don't even remember what happened in the last week because it's so muddled up with the ordinary busyness of motherhood.

Monotony can be disheartening. There are times when I have to put on my cap of duty and just get the bathroom cleaned. Or when I'm tired of taking my boys to the same places to play over and over again. Sometimes it feels as if I just planned my meals yesterday and now I already have to think about what we'll eat this week and then shop for it all. Again.

I spend the majority of my time taking care of my family and my home. I tell my boys to stop fighting, and fifteen minutes later I'm saying it again. I begin the evening's meal preparation, even though I just put away dishes from our previous meal. Caretaking involves a litany of repetitive tasks: changing diapers, infant feedings, nap schedules (if you have one), getting children out the door in time for school, homework, baths, and bedtime routines. Every day is fundamentally the same.

THE BEAUTY OF REPETITION

When it comes to our everyday tasks, life can feel very ordinary—not so special or exciting. We live in a culture that values and lives for the big and exciting things of life, such as new babies, weddings, family vacations, or a big birthday party. These are the moments we capture on Instagram.

Repetition has a way of blurring our days together. It can make everything feel colorless and faded, and as if those bigger exciting moments are the only splashes of color. But what if we're underestimating these ordinary days and repetitive tasks? What if we're missing something? The mundane moments of motherhood are difficult, but the mundane beauties can be missed: cuddling on the couch to read a book together, having heart-to-heart talks, spotting an act of kindness between siblings, praying together, and talking about Jesus and the gospel. These are all sweet parts of this repetition. These are ordinary moments for eternity.

We need to discover how to spot these daily beauties and cherish them—because God created them. He made repetition.

Think about our world for a moment. Every day the sun rises and sets; every day the moon waxes or wanes; and every day these acts praise their Creator. In his book *Orthodoxy*, G.K. Chesterton mentions how the repetition of the sun's rising might not be due to a lifelessness but to a rush of life. Chesterton compares the repetition found in nature to a child's enjoyment in repeating the same games and songs. He says children do this because they have "fierce and free spirits"; their joy in repetition is due to an excess of life, not an absence.

Chesterton then says:

> *For grown-up people are not strong enough to exult*
> *in monotony. But perhaps God is strong enough*
> *to exult in monotony. It is possible that God says*
> *every morning, "Do it again" to the sun; and every*
> *evening, "Do it again" to the moon. It may not be*
> *automatic necessity that makes all daisies alike;*
> *it may be that God makes every daisy separately,*
> *but has never got tired of making them. It may be*
> *that he has the eternal appetite of infancy ... The*
> *repetition in Nature may not be a mere recurrence;*
> *it may be a theatrical encore.*

Orthodoxy, p 92

The act of repetition can be a thing of beauty all by itself. For example, we're called to repeat the sacrament of the Lord's Supper as a church body (1 Corinthians 11 v 23-25), and as we repeat this act, it becomes imprinted upon us—informing us about Christ and about ourselves. We're teaching ourselves the gospel over and over. As we know from observing our children, things must be repeated if they are to be learned. So, we must come again and again to the communion table—and to worship, prayer, and God's word—if we are to become more like Jesus.

Someday we'll be more fully like God and no longer grow tired of repetition. We will have the "eternal appetite of infancy", as Chesterton expressed it, and will exult in the joyful repetition of worship. We'll cry, "Encore!" every time we worship the Lamb of God, who was slain for our sins. Until then, we are given tastes of this beauty here on earth as we repeat our tasks of mothering.

LITTLE THINGS

It's the little things we are called to. Day in and day out. Minute by minute. These little moments that can feel so monotonous have the power to shape you and your children. This poem by Julie A.F. Carney called *Little Things* (partly quoted here), which I've read with my own children, is a great reminder of this:

> *Little drops of water,*
> *Little grains of sand,*
> *Make the mighty ocean*
> *And the pleasant land.*
> *So the little moments,*
> *Humble though they be,*
> *Make the mighty ages*
> *Of Eternity.*
>
> *Gyo Fujikawa, A Child's Book of Poems, p 89*

Just as many tiny droplets make up one vast ocean, so all of our days are made up of tiny moments. We don't always see the bigger picture when we're teaching our children a Bible verse, or probing their hearts, or spending time with them. Capturing the little things is what motherhood is about. When we train our children (talk to them, ask searching questions, and then pray with them)—or when we instruct them in God's word and help them apply it to the every-day struggles in their lives—then we are capturing the little things that will add up to big things. This is the glory found in the mundane. These are the most important times. May we be ever mindful of the Spirit's work in these seemingly insignificant moments.

When we read the Bible, we see the Holy Spirit move in miraculous and seemingly impossible ways. His ways seem so big and exciting. But for us moms today, the majority of the time, we will see the Holy Spirit work in little things. He works on us and our children moment by moment, day by day, little by little. He is changing us one step at a time. He is working through our repetitive tasks to change our hearts and the hearts of our children. He is working through every Bible verse, every moment of instruction, every prayer, every conversation. He works through our actions of serving care and nurturing kindness (even in the times when our heart attitude doesn't match our actions).

Feeding your child when they are hungry, changing a dirty diaper, bathing your child, and scrubbing the dishes all show your child Christ-like service. You provide their first glimpse of the Savior. But we don't always see that until those little workings of the Spirit bear fruit and grow into something bigger (Galatians 5 v 22-23). We have to have faith in the Spirit's work when we can't see the big picture in the ordinary moments of motherhood. We can ask the Holy Spirit for help, so we can remain steadfast and faithful in the mundane tasks before us every day.

PLANTING SEEDS

My two sons and I recently did a seed study for school. We buried twelve bean seeds in individual sections of an egg carton. Inside those seemingly insignificant seeds were all the information and tools necessary for growth into flourishing plants. On the outside it looked as if nothing was happening, but inside the seed was already slowly changing.

Thinking about the small, ordinary aspects of motherhood as seeds we are sowing every day is helpful. Reading about other mothers in history has helped me in this. For instance, Elizabeth Scatliffe Newton—the mother of the famous eighteenth-century British hymnwriter, preacher, and abolitionist John Newton—planted early seeds in John's heart.

John was her only child, and Elizabeth suffered from tuberculosis. Though Elizabeth spent much of her time in bed, she never squandered her years with John. By the time John was four he could read and repeat his catechisms and his children's hymns.

When John was only seven, tuberculosis claimed his mother's life. This young man, who eventually wrote the hymn "Amazing Grace," would first travel deep into his own depravity and wickedness before Jesus opened his blind eyes.

When John later looked back at his life, he gave credit to his mother:

Though in process of time I sinned away all the advantages of these early impressions, yet they were for a great while a restraint upon me; they returned again and again, and it was very long before I could wholly shake them off; and when the Lord at length opened my eyes, I found a great benefit from the recollection of them.

Later, John would say:

My dear mother, besides the pains she took with me, often commended me with many prayers and tears to God; and I doubt not but I reap the fruits of these prayers to this hour.

What a hopeful testimony from a son about his mother. Even if you have children under seven, every little moment matters. All the small ways in which you point your children to Christ plant seeds in their little hearts and minds. You just have to trust God with the growth and the fruit.

CALLED TO THE PROCESS

Math is not my forte. As an English major in college I tried to get out of as many math credits as possible. It wasn't always the concepts that frustrated me; it was the process: all those long complicated steps that it took to solve one problem. I wanted to rush past the means and arrive quickly at the end. Don't we all, to some extent, try to do this in our own lives?

We would rather skip the process if we could. But this is the process that Scripture calls us to in our own spiritual lives and in the lives of our children.

> *And I am sure of this, that he who began a good work in you will bring it to completion at the day of Jesus Christ.*
>
> *Philippians 1 v 6*

Once we are saved in Christ and believe in him by faith, we are seeking (with the help of the Holy Spirit and our church family) to live lives that are continually in the process of change (1 Peter 1 v 2). We are called to become more and more like Jesus, more and more dependent on the Spirit, and more and more aware of our sinfulness and God's holiness, and to be trained in a faith that deepens through trials (James 1 v 2-4). God has already declared us holy through the sacrifice of Christ (Hebrews 10 v 14). But we are continually becoming more and more what God already declares us to be: *holy.*

> *So we do not lose heart. Though our outer self is wasting away, our inner self is being renewed day by day. For this light momentary affliction is preparing for us an eternal weight of glory beyond all comparison.*
>
> *2 Corinthians 4 v 16-17*

As we saw in chapter 1, the troubles of living out the small ordinary moments of motherhood are preparing for us a glory to come in heaven, because God is using them to renew us inwardly day by day. He is using the small mundane moments of motherhood to refine us and make us more like Jesus. Every act of disobedience, every bad attitude from our children, is being used by God to make us more patient. He is using us to plant seeds into the hearts of our children (who are also in a process of change), but the behavior of our children is also showing us who we really are and how desperately we need a Savior and a helper in the Holy Spirit.

Our children need grace, but *we* need so much grace as well. The Spirit is using our parenting to shape and refine our children, but he's also using our children to shape and refine us, which in turn affects our parenting. It's a circle of grace. We don't see it now, but the process of being refined through the mundanity of motherhood will reap a harvest of fruit in our own lives as well as our children's.

RENEWAL TO TRANSFORMATION

John Newton's mother couldn't see into the future for her son, let alone control it. But there was still fruit reaped from her faithful little seeds. And though the repetitive tasks and small ordinary things of motherhood can be grueling, or maybe even seem pointless, if you remain steadfast and "do not lose heart," you will see a plentiful harvest: the harvest of a renewed heart as a mother and, hopefully, spiritual fruit in the hearts of your children (even if there are seasons of rebellion and straying).

But beyond these things, there will be a harvest in heaven. God will one day say to you, "Well done, good and faithful servant" (Matthew 25 v 23). And even if you didn't see the harvest you wanted on earth, you will most assuredly see it from the higher and holier perspective of heaven. Furthermore, if you are a mom who feels like a failure in these things, bring it to Jesus in prayer and ask for the Spirit's help. For all moms who belong to Christ, there will be an eternal glory, and all areas of failure will be redeemed. And his mundane means of renewing you day by day, though it made you tired and weary, will result in a final transformation, when you'll be what you were truly meant to be all along, and you will have the joy of seeing the Lord face to face.

FOR YOUR HEART AND LIFE

This week, as you are doing something repetitive and mundane (washing the dishes, cooking dinner, changing the baby's diaper, or helping with homework), think about the beauty and purpose God might have for you in that moment. Maybe even stick this poem on a post-it note in one or more of the places around the house where you do these mundane tasks:

> *Little drops of water,*
> *Little grains of sand,*
> *Make the mighty ocean*
> *And the pleasant land.*
> *So the little moments,*
> *Humble though they be,*
> *Make the mighty ages*
> *Of Eternity.*

Dear Jesus,

Thank you that you have a plan for all the little moments of my life and the lives of my children. Help me to see the glory that you see in the ordinary things that feel so mundane and boring to me. Help me to see the bigger picture in the repetition of my days and to have the joy of Christ as I live them out. Thank you for working in me little by little every day, and I pray that you will do the same for my children as you give me strength to parent them. Please continue to give me the patience and perseverance I need to be faithful in the mundane moments of motherhood.

In your name, Amen

Journaling Space

CHAPTER 3

Rest Releases Our Burdens

Prone to wander, Lord, I feel it,
Prone to leave the God I love.
Here's my heart, oh, take and seal it,
Seal it for thy courts above.

The words have barely rolled off my tongue as I bend down to hear my three-year-old son whisper in my ear, "Mama, I want a snack." My hands feel around diapers, wipes, and extra clothing items in my bag and then grab onto a small packet of crackers. I tear open the packet and hand it to my son as I resume singing.

Come, my Lord, no longer tarry,
Take my ransomed soul away;
Send thine angels now to carry
Me to realms of endless day.

I glance down to see my son huddled over his blue sneakers, tugging at the yellow laces that have come untied. As I continue to sing one of my favorite hymns, I plop him down on a chair to retie his shoes.

This is a typical Sunday morning service for young moms—worship as a mother. We sing praise with our mouths to God, while worshiping by tearing open cracker packets and tying loose laces. It's Sunday: a Sabbath day for many—a day to rest, take it easy, be refreshed, and prepare for another week of schedules, appointments, and work. And yet my hands are busy at work all day. How can I enjoy rest when caring and nurturing is a round-the-clock job?

DOING IT ALL

When I was a first-time mom, I thought I should be able to do everything on my own: take care of my baby while also doing the dishes, cleaning, cooking, and keeping on top of the laundry pile. I even felt that it was wrong if I wanted to have a break from my child. It felt weak to ask for help. It showed my true state: that I wasn't Supermom.

Pictures from Pinterest showed me all the perfect crafts, beautifully decorated living rooms, and homemade cleaning supplies, as if this was the norm for all competent moms. The posts on social media can make comparison an issue for many moms. Most of us are posting the happy highlights of our lives, which don't give a full picture of a home and family. Even posting "real" photos like a messy room or a not-so-flattering selfie are a far cry from showing the multi-faceted and emotional life of a human being. We'll never give others a true taste of our imperfections from a bad hair day or unfolded laundry.

There is a gap between the reality of lived-out parenthood and the images and statuses we see on social media. But God doesn't "like" these posts as we do: he looks at them differently. He knows the whole picture; he searches and knows hearts. He knows reality. We already have his stamp of approval in our lives through his Son Jesus. So, we can come to the end of our social-media selves and realize that we worship the Son of God and not picture perfect circumstances.

I began to see this faulty thinking sometime after my second son came along. Taking care of a baby and a toddler showed me that I couldn't sustain this way of living. I knew I needed to cut back, take it easy, not burden myself, and not feel bad about asking for help. This realization happened slowly over time when I began to feel so overwhelmed that I couldn't take it anymore, and I knew something was wrong.

Even now, as a mother of three small children, I often feel the burdens of everything in my life. Just because I learned my lesson with baby number two doesn't mean I don't still struggle with trying to be strong on my own and do everything by myself. I easily fall back to those old patterns. I can feel burdened, I feel overwhelmed at times, I break down, I cry, I get angry, I feel sad. It seems as if everything is riding on my shoulders: that I'm the one spinning all the plates in our family—and that can be emotionally and mentally draining. I know that many moms can relate to this mindset. We are burdened women.

ACCEPTING LIMITATIONS

In all my efforts to be Supermom, I forget I'm only human. I can't be all knowing, all seeing, all powerful, or in more than one place at a time. In fact, those are attributes that belong to God alone! There is only one true God, and I am not him. He is the one truly spinning all the plates, and not just in my life but the whole world. I am human, and I am a sinner. I don't need to pretend otherwise. I can admit this to myself and to my family, and even ask for forgiveness when necessary. Because I am human, I only have so much patience and so much strength. Ever heard of reaching your limit? I think, as moms, we come to that place more times than we can count. Especially single moms, who are left navigating family and work all alone.

At times like this, it's good to remember that the Christian faith isn't for those who are strong and good enough but for those who are weak and foolish.

> *But God chose what is foolish in the world to shame*
> *the wise; God chose what is weak in the world*
> *to shame the strong; God chose what is low and*
> *despised in the world, even things that are not, to*
> *bring to nothing things that are, so that no human*
> *being might boast in the presence of God.*
> *1 Corinthians 1 v 27-29*

We tend to forget that this portion of Scripture is referring to all of us: to *all* those called by God in Christ. He is building an army of weaklings to show his strength and power through us. Just as when God whittled down Gideon's army from 32,000 to 300 men (Judges 7 v 2-8), the Lord is showing that it is not by human might that we receive victory but through the power of God alone.

It is the mark of true humility to accept and remind ourselves of these truths about our limited creatureliness and God's infinite power. God knows all these things of motherhood are beyond us, and so in humility we must seek after him. Humility is remembering who we truly are and who God is: *he* is the Creator, and *we* are the created. The freedom of rest that accompanies this truth is what we need. You don't need to be a tough, strong, supermom but just a humble mom who knows her true place. When you begin to humbly rely on the strength of the Spirit, and not your own strength, you will find the peace you were always meant to have.

HE IS OUR REST

Resting around my house can be quite difficult. My two boys don't take naps anymore (only my little girl), and the only time I feel that I can get away is through handheld devices and copious amounts of snacks. But of course I can't do that for too long or I feel guilty. So, it feels as if there is no true rest for me. But I forget that rest is ultimately rooted in a particular person.

Mary was acquainted with this person. In the biblical account of Mary and Martha, Mary found her rest at the feet of Jesus. Her sister, Martha, however, was engaged in anxious toil.

Now as they went on their way, Jesus entered a village. And a woman named Martha welcomed him into her house. And she had a sister called Mary, who sat at the Lord's feet and listened to his teaching. But Martha was distracted with much serving. And she went up to him and said, "Lord, do you not care that my sister has left me to serve alone? Tell her then to help me." But the Lord answered her, "Martha, Martha, you are anxious and troubled about many things, but one thing is necessary. Mary has chosen the good portion, which will not be taken away from her."

Luke 10 v 38-42

As moms it would be so easy for us to side with Martha. We are "distracted with much serving," because we have to be. Though Martha asks Jesus to reprimand her sister (v 40), Martha is the one who gets the reprimand. "Martha, Martha, you are anxious and troubled about many things, but one thing is necessary. Mary has chosen the good portion, which will not be taken away from her" (v 41-42).

Jesus flips things around in his usual way. So, the woman sitting around doing nothing is right and the woman serving is wrong? It's perplexing at first—and we can understand Martha's frustration—until we see what Jesus is getting at. Martha's serving was good, but she was not operating out of a place of rest. As moms it's normal for us to be "anxious and troubled about many things." We can worry about our children's behavior, their future, their education, or their eating habits. We can worry about the state of our homes, the state of our bank accounts, and our success in life and mothering. But Jesus stops us and asks, *Have you chosen the good portion?*

And in all the anxious toil of motherhood, he reminds us that only one thing is necessary amid all the craziness: *himself.*

We learn rest from the one who is rest. When we heap the heavy mothering burdens of the day or week on our shoulders, Jesus tells us this:

> *Come to me, all who labor and are heavy laden,*
> *and I will give you rest. Take my yoke upon you, and*
> *learn from me, for I am gentle and lowly in heart,*
> *and you will find rest for your souls. For my yoke is*
> *easy, and my burden is light.*
>
> *Matthew 11 v 28-30*

The burdens we put on ourselves as moms can be crushing, but Jesus tells us to come and learn from him. What are we learning from him? To be gentle and lowly in heart. This is how we find rest in him: when we stop thinking everything is up to us and dependent on our success as moms. His yoke is easy and light for us, because he has put everything on his own shoulders. Our rest is found in putting our burdens on the one who was meant to carry them for us. Rest in Christ is the place where the burdened find their freedom. We find rest by being humbly dependent on our Creator. He's got this. Not us.

JESUS SHOWS MOMS THE WAY

The ministry of Jesus is instructive for mothers looking for rest. Jesus had a busy ministry, a demanding job, but he understood the finite part of himself and realized that he had human needs. In an article from her blog, Vaneetha Rendall Risner says this:

Jesus never seemed hurried, though he was inundated by people with urgent needs. Much of the time he was surrounded by crowds, with barely enough time to catch his breath. Events happened quickly, tumbling one after the other. He went from preaching in a synagogue to casting out a demon to healing a sick friend to ministering to the whole city gathered at his door at sundown. And this was just one day!

crosswalk.com

After this one day of chaos, we read this:

Very early in the morning, while it was still dark, he departed and went out to a desolate place, and there he prayed.

Mark 1 v 35

Vaneetha goes on to say, "After ministering to others, and before pouring himself out again, Jesus left everyone and spent time with God. This pattern is repeated throughout the Gospels."

Elsewhere, Jesus encourages his disciples to rest (Mark 6 v 31-32). And Jesus even took a nap in a boat (Mark 4 v 35-41). Jesus modeled for us how we should live within our limits as flesh-and-blood created beings. He showed us physical rest, spiritual rest, and mental rest—even, and especially, when life is overwhelming and busy. When the crowds demanded to see Jesus, he was not afraid to step away and leave (Mark 1 v 37-38). He specifically chose what groups he was going to teach, meaning he had to say no to some (Luke 4 v 43).

I have a tendency to push myself, and keep going in all I do, and I only seek a "time out" or break for myself when I feel that I really need it. But the danger with this is that I'll find myself able to stick it out for a long period of time, but then I just have a mental and emotional breakdown. I'll finally get to a point where I can't take it anymore—mentally, emotionally, or physically. I'll keep going until I'm exhausted. I know this is not wisdom and not humility. Vaneetha Rendall Risner reminds me of this when she says that "denying myself physical rest is not a virtue. It is a form of pride."

This can be hard to notice by ourselves, so it's helpful to invite a Christian friend to observe your life and let you know if they spot anything of concern. They may need to tell you that you are pushing yourself too hard and must build in rest before it's too late. They may even recognise that you are struggling mentally and need some help from your pastor or a health professional. Or they may be able to reassure you that your life is "normal" for a mom with a young child, but that they will pray for you to be able to keep going.

When I keep pushing myself and striving in my own strength, I only last for so long, until some part of me breaks down. I'm finally realizing that I need to safeguard and prioritise my times of rest for myself on a regular basis (even if I'm feeling ok), and that this is a sign of wisdom and humility and is not lazy, selfish, or irresponsible. True rest, when taken well in a spirit of humility, only helps us be less of these negative things. We must work hard and be faithful as mothers but also engage in a rhythm of rest for ourselves alongside work. Jesus shows us how.

HUMBLE AND PRAYERFUL DEPENDENCE

God brings seasons in my life when I come to the end of myself and I can't ride through on my own strength. I finally feel my need. I draw near to God and cry out for the Spirit's help on a regular basis.

But, to be honest, when I'm not in emotional-crisis mode, I easily fall back into self-reliance. One practical way I do this is by not praying enough. I often don't ask the Holy Spirit for help in my parenting or to work in the lives of my children, my husband, and myself. Then I eventually feel burdened and drained because I'm not leaning on him. Prayer expresses our dependency on God. A lack of prayer shows self-sufficiency. I am often guilty of this. Maybe you are too?

One practical way we find rest, one way we humble ourselves, one way we cast our burdens on him, is through prayer.

> *Do not be anxious about anything, but in everything by prayer and supplication with thanksgiving let your requests be made known to God. And the peace of God, which surpasses all understanding, will guard your hearts and your minds in Christ Jesus.*
> *Philippians 4 v 6-7*

Are you feeling overwhelmed? Burdened? Anxious?

Pray.

God promises to hear his children when we pray (Proverbs 15 v 29).

God created us to be dependent on him, and when we fight against this by striving in our own strength, then we are actually weakening ourselves. We were made to be limited, and yet we act as if we are not, so we have strife within ourselves. We can't find rest. True humility will bring us back to God's design for our dependence, and back to peace and rest in him. Wonderfully, this leads to not just surviving but flourishing. It's my pride and self-reliance that make me feel as if I'm the one holding it all together for my family. Instead of acting and feeling as if I am the savior of my family, I need to prayerfully rely on the strong and loving hands of the true Savior.

Another way, besides prayer, that we can humbly rely on the Spirit is through physical rest. This can mean leaving some things undone in order to get a good night's sleep, lying down for a nap at midday, going for a refreshing walk, getting some time alone to recharge, or engaging in a hobby. When we choose these forms of rest, it's an act of trust because we are relinquishing control. We're saying, "I've done what I can; now I leave the rest up to you, God." This way we remember that it's not all up to us to keep things moving in the household. We can entrust our homes to God.

Jesus has conquered our enemies of pride and self-reliance. They went with him to the cross and the tomb, but they were left buried and dead when he rose from the grave. Why would we continue to rely on things that are dead and buried—things that are enemies to our spiritual lives? Pride and self-reliance do not give life to us. Only in returning to the one who gives us rest will we truly flourish (Isaiah 30 v 15).

FREEDOM FOR THE BURDENED

I no longer think it's weak to ask for help, but a humble strength. I need to be quick to rely on those in my local church, and rely on the Holy Spirit, to help me carry my burdens. I'm not perfect at this, but I'm more aware and willing to move in this direction. For me, this has meant asking for help from my husband or from others in my community. I have made priorities in every season, cutting back and saying no when things feel like they might be too much. Laying my burdens down at the feet of Jesus has also meant asking for and relying on his strength to help me, while repenting of my pride and self-sufficiency. True freedom is found in humble reliance on God and bringing him our burdens through prayer. It's trusting in the truth that he is in control and not us. Being aware of our limitations, and accepting them, is also a form of humility and a launching pad for more rest and reliance on our Savior.

When you come to the end of your strength, Jesus is there waiting. Your burdens may be crushing and demanding; they are wicked taskmasters spouting out lies. Pride and self-reliance put these burdens on us. But Jesus wants you to come to him. He wants you to lay your burdens down at his feet, and then he'll place his lighter burden upon you: the "burden" of righteousness that he won for you. His burden is easy and light because it's the burden of humility and not pride. It's the burden of rest and trust in the God who carries you, me, and the whole universe in his hands.

FOR YOUR HEART AND LIFE

This week set apart a specific time to think and plan out a way to incorporate a rhythm of rest into your life, whether that's scheduling a consistent time to get away (however that looks for you and fits into your life), finding a good time to study and pray, joining a book club or Bible study, taking a class, etc. Invite one person from your local church in on the thinking and planning. Get their advice and have them keep you accountable.

Dear Jesus,

Forgive me for relying on my strength alone. I often forget that I am limited and you are more than enough. Help me to remember that you are God over my life and I am not. I come to you with my burdens and place them at your feet. I know you will give me strength by the power of the Holy Spirit. Give me the courage to be humble enough to ask for help. And give me the grace to trust you more. I need your rest. I need you.

In your name,

Amen

Journaling Space

CHAPTER 4

"Weak and Needy"
Is Perfect

Just when I think my house is clean, sunlight pours in through the windows. Then I see every little crumb, stain, and speck of dust. The difference sunlight makes to my floors always takes me by surprise. How can the contrast be so great between dark and light? Imperfections are rarely seen in the dark. And yet they were always there: the sun is just showing the reality.

In much the same way, God uses motherhood as a light in our lives to see the reality about ourselves. At times, motherhood is so hard that it can make us feel inadequate and insecure, because we're finally seeing how helpless and needy we actually are. It's showing us that we are more sinful than we ever thought. All human beings are in this condition before God—whether we are moms or not—but we don't always see it. We sometimes have the lights off in our lives, until God decides to use something to shine light in those dark places.

This is actually his love and mercy at work in our lives. He doesn't just save us and then leave us to figure this whole Christianity thing out for ourselves. God is actively helping us, teaching us, and training us. These are his means of freeing us from our own sinful shackles and providing us with more joy in this life. There is a loving purpose in the humbling aspects of motherhood.

BEING NEEDY ISN'T A SIN

Before sin entered the world, we were already needy. Adam and Eve were sinless but still needed help in many ways. God sustained their lives through food, breath, and beating hearts. They needed fellowship with God in order to flourish. In her book, *None Like Him*, Jen Wilkin says:

> *God created them* [Adam and Eve] *needy, that in their need they might turn to the Source of all that is needful, acknowledge their need, and worship. Instead, they angled for autonomy.*
>
> *p 62*

Not feeling needy is actually when we are most needy. I know, for myself, that self-sufficiency gets in the way of me feeling my need for the Spirit. I think I'm strong enough on my own to check off my to-do list. I think I'm ultimately in charge of my household when really it's God who holds us all together. The most dangerous place in which we can find ourselves, as mothers, is in thinking that we don't need help, that we are good enough, and that we are strong enough. It's really when we feel most weak and needy that we are strong, because that's when God's grace shines brightest. The Spirit works perfectly through our weakness.

He's humbling us to make us more dependent on him and therefore more in line with how we were designed. As Jen Wilkin goes on to say:

> *Sanctification is the process of learning increasing dependence, not autonomy.*

God designed us to need him, and when we act as if we don't, then it's to our own peril and misery. When we repent and return to God's original design for us, then we have a taste of his peace and rest.

MOTHERHOOD HUMBLES US

Children are a loving gift from our gracious God, so motherhood is always something to be thankful for. But motherhood is also good for us because it shows us who we really are and who God truly is. Being a mom is like letting in those sunbeams that highlight the mess in our hearts that we didn't know was there.

For me, motherhood has shown me how I struggle with anger and impatience. Before motherhood, I wouldn't have pegged those as big issues in my life. Being a mom not only showed me this but has trained me as well. Motherhood has been my teacher and coach in greater patience, love, grace, and dependence.

Of course, it's really the Holy Spirit doing these things, but in moms he's using motherhood as the vehicle.

I've felt helpless at times in the face of my eldest son's anxiety. I saw it and felt it in him when he was as young as two years old, though I didn't know what to name it back then. I just thought his behavior was strange. I waited for him to outgrow it, but it only seemed to change form and expressions as he got older. There were good seasons and bad seasons, ups and downs. When I started realizing that it was anxiety, I knew that what my son experienced wasn't the average child's form of fear and anxiety. I knew it was something more and that he wouldn't outgrow it. We always looked at Scriptures about anxiety with him, we would always pray with him, and we would always speak truth into his fears, but I felt that he might need additional help; and I felt that I needed help too.

So I reached out to leaders in our church to get advice and ask for prayer as we began to seek out therapy for our son. My church family still checks in on us to see how things are going, and they volunteer to pray for us. His Sunday School teachers have specifically prayed for him as well and have seen growth during his most recent year in class. The help and prayers of my church family have been hugely important to me and my husband as we seek to support our son. They don't dismiss us for being needy. They love us, support us, and pray for us.

I didn't always know how to deal with our son's unpredictable behavior. Sometimes I handled it well; sometimes I didn't. Sometimes I just felt at a loss. But it was during this period of acute helplessness that God used a Bible story to comfort me. I was reading to my boys the story of Jesus walking on water (Matthew 14 v 22-33). One of the central characters is the disciple Peter. When Peter saw Jesus walking on the water, he wanted to walk on the water too, and he was able to, so long as he kept his eyes on Jesus. But once Peter took his eyes off Jesus and looked at the terrifying storm around him, he began to sink. It was Jesus who stopped him from drowning when he pulled Peter up from the raging sea. As I came to that part of the story, I felt the comfort of the Holy Spirit saying, *I will not let him sink.*

Jesus is with my son in his anxiety. And I am not the one who can stop him from sinking. It is Jesus himself (who loves my son dearly) who will reach out to help him. I'm striving to be faithful to help my son as much as humanly possible until he leaves my care. I want him to be well equipped to cope and deal with his anxiety in healthy and biblical ways for the rest of his life. But as he goes out on his own and walks those waves, I have to trust Jesus to be there to save my son from sinking. I know he is in good hands and that his loving Father loves him in ways I will never be able to. I can't change my son's heart—but I can trust in the one who can.

WE'RE ALL FAILURES, BUT FOR ONE

In the early stages of my third pregnancy I was fighting daily nausea and fatigue. Every afternoon I would sit my boys down with snacks and a show, and tell them not to bother me as I slept. A few times I would wake up to my toddler jumping on me. One of these times I yelled at him. He cried and reached his arms out for me to hold him. I held him and told him, "I'm sorry. What mama did was wrong. Please forgive me."

I wish this was the only time I've ever yelled at my children, but it's not. I wish I'd never had to see the hurt in their eyes or the disappointment etched on their faces when I'm sinning. But I've told both of my sons, many times, that mama is a sinner like them and that only Jesus is without sin.

The cross makes everyone level: all are failures before him. We all fall short, and yet God *chose* us.

> *Brothers and sisters, think of what you were when*
> *you were called. Not many of you were wise by*
> *human standards; not many were influential; not*
> *many were of noble birth. But God chose the foolish*
> *things of the world to shame the wise; God chose the*
> *weak things of the world to shame the strong. God*
> *chose the lowly things of this world and the despised*
> *things—and the things that are not—to nullify the*
> *things that are, so that no one may boast before him.*
> *It is because of him that you are in Christ Jesus, who*
> *has become for us wisdom from God—that is, our*
> *righteousness, holiness and redemption. Therefore,*
> *as it is written: "Let the one who boasts boast in the*
> *Lord."*
>
> *1 Corinthians 1 v 26-31 (NIV)*

God didn't choose us because we never fail; he chose us because *he* never fails. He is good, kind, loving, and merciful, and that is why he saved us. So we don't boast in ourselves, but we boast in him. The cross of Christ levels us and ultimately declares us all failures. But Jesus came to not fail in our place. And as he breathed his final breath, and then breathed a new resurrected one, his failure-free life became our own.

So now we can parent in the midst of failures, knowing that we are fully known by God and accepted fully through Christ. We can take our burdens of guilt to him, ask for his forgiveness, and ask the Spirit to help us change. After that there is no condemnation (Romans 8 v 1). We can even come to him again and again with our failures, knowing that his mercy and grace never run dry.

Our failures are just another opportunity to boast in the Lord. As a mom, I can use my failures of anger and impatience to point my children to one who is perfect for them: one who will never fail them because he died for them.

Jesus is my children's ultimate hope in this life. Though I am his representative to them, I'm an imperfect one. So my prayer is that my children will see me for who I really am and look to Christ as one who is greater. I can tell them that he is the one who nailed my failures to a tree and can do the same for them.

OUR GOOD AND HIS GLORY

Not only are our failures meant to throw us at the feet of the failure-free Savior, but they are being used in our lives for our good and his glory. God uses our failures to show that he is strong, and he uses them to humble us.

> *But he gives more grace. Therefore [Scripture] says, "God opposes the proud but gives grace to the humble."* James 4 v 6

Humble yourselves, therefore, under the mighty hand
of God so that at the proper time he may exalt you.

1 Peter 5 v 6

As moms, we can freely admit our weakness instead of hiding who we are, because of the grace of God. After all, grace is made available to the humble. Until we recognize that we're needy, we won't see our need for grace.

Jesus even said:

Those who are well have no need of a physician, but
those who are sick. I came not to call the righteous,
but sinners.

Mark 2 v 17

Jesus came to earth to rescue sinful mothers in need of grace. If we think we are healthy enough on our own, then we spurn his grace and don't live in the reality of who we are now, in and through Christ. If we want the power of Christ to rest upon our mothering, we must boast in him alone. God wants to work in us as much as he does in our children. He puts us in the daily grind of motherhood so that he can purify us and enable us to parent our children better. He wants us to see and confess our sin toward our children so we can be a real-life example to them of what a true follower of Christ is. A true follower of Christ doesn't have it all together and is not a star parent. A true follower of Christ walks humbly with God (Micah 6 v 8).

Our failures as moms can bring glory to God and can be for our benefit if we do the right thing with them: if we don't hide our failings or cover them up but instead draw attention to them, so that we can rightly cast them off. This way, we and our children can know that these failings are wrong and not part of the life of a believer. This helps us, it helps our children, and it brings glory to God by showing his greatness and perfection towards his own children. He is glorified in our humility because it reveals who he really is—the only sinless one.

GOD RAISES US UP

So once we feel the humbling effects of motherhood, what then? You don't have to fight the feeling that you aren't enough. You can take it to God, who *is* enough. You can pour out your heart to him, knowing that with him you will not be easily shaken (Psalm 62 v 2). You can trust him as your rock and your refuge in the humbling moments of motherhood (Psalm 62 v 6-7) because he has told us:

> *I dwell in the high and holy place,*
> *and also with him who is of a contrite and lowly*
> *spirit,*
> *to revive the spirit of the lowly,*
> *and to revive the heart of the contrite.*
>
> Isaiah 57 v 15

In this verse, God promises that he is close to those who are humble. Or another way to put it is this: *our humility is what brings us closer to God.* Greater dependence on him equals greater intimacy. When God raises us up, we are more in touch with the Spirit's power in our lives because we aren't relying on ourselves alone but on the Lord, who draws us in closer when we humbly admit and accept our dependence on him. He is the source of our reviving. When motherhood has made us low, we look to him to raise us up. The Holy Spirit is our helper; he will provide our strength.

> *Have you not known? Have you not heard?*
> *The LORD is the everlasting God,*
>   *the Creator of the ends of the earth.*
> *He does not faint or grow weary;*
>   *his understanding is unsearchable.*
> *He gives power to the faint,*
>   *and to him who has no might he increases*
>   *strength.*
> *Even youths shall faint and be weary,*
>   *and young men* [young moms!] *shall fall*
>   *exhausted;*
> *but they who wait for the LORD shall renew their*
>   *strength;*
>   *they shall mount up with wings like eagles;*
> *they shall run and not be weary;*
>   *they shall walk and not faint.*
>
>   *Isaiah 40 v 28-31*

We can't be raised up by his grace and power until we are humbled. The depths are the way to the heights. This is God's plan for our motherhood.

In Luke 14, Jesus was at the home of a religious leader. He saw how some of the guests were taking the best seats so he told them a parable about a wedding feast:

When you are invited by someone to a wedding feast,
do not sit down in a place of honor, lest someone
more distinguished than you be invited by him,
and he who invited you both will come and say to
you, "Give your place to this person," and then you
will begin with shame to take the lowest place. But
when you are invited, go and sit in the lowest place,
so that when your host comes he may say to you,
"Friend, move up higher." Then you will be honored
in the presence of all who sit at table with you. For
everyone who exalts himself will be humbled, and he
who humbles himself will be exalted.

Luke 14 v 8-11

This parable might seem as if it has nothing to do with motherhood, but the danger of taking the seat of honor in our lives is still there. We put ourselves in this seat when we think that being a good mom is accomplished by our self-effort and strength, and our ability to juggle everything. It won't be long until we are put to shame and must take the lower seat at the table. We aren't ultimately in charge of our lives or our children's lives—that seat belongs to God alone. He sits at the head of the table. But when we remember that we are lowly and are willing to take the low seat at the table, we will never be put to shame. Instead God will say, *Come, my child; sit closer to me.*

Our God lifts up the humble. He will never turn you away when you come to him in need. He welcomes the weak and is a friend to the needy. When he shines his light into your dark places, it's done not to shame you but to love you. Just as we discipline our children because we love them, so God disciplines us out of love (Proverbs 3 v 12). He's bringing you back to the happy place of humble dependence on him: the place he intended for you from the beginning, even before sin entered the world.

FOR YOUR HEART AND LIFE

This week try an upcycling or small rehab project, or consider fixing something that is broken. Take before and after pictures to remind yourself of how God takes our neediness and failure and uses them to change us for our good and his glory.

 Dear Jesus,

Thank you for not leaving me to myself, but instead using motherhood to show me my need for you. Help me to remember how you designed me for humble dependence. Show me how to come back to your design for my life, and may your Spirit give me grace to humble myself and remember that you are in control. Forgive me taking the seat of honor at times, instead of the low and needy place at your table. Thank you for coming close to me in my need and not rejecting me. I know you will help me.

Amen

Journaling Space

CHAPTER 5

When Mom Is Called to Suffer

I t's a struggle to be a mom. We all know it's hard. But some moms are called to suffer in particular ways, and it affects their mothering. For these moms, daily "deaths" are complicated, messy, and harder than for the average mother. These are the moms battling postpartum depression and/or anxiety, living with chronic illness, going through a crisis, or raising a child (or children) with unique challenges, such as autism, chronic illness or a physical disability.

These are the moms who know what it means to "go to the garden," as Jesus did in the Garden of Gethsemane:

> *Then Jesus went with them to a place called Gethsemane, and he said to his disciples, "Sit here, while I go over there and pray." And taking with him Peter and the two sons of Zebedee, he began to be sorrowful and troubled. Then he said to them, "My soul is very sorrowful, even to death; remain*

> *here, and watch with me." And going a little farther*
> *he fell on his face and prayed, saying, "My Father, if*
> *it be possible, let this cup pass from me; nevertheless,*
> *not as I will, but as you will."*
>
> *Matthew 26 v 36-39*

Jesus went to the garden before he went to the cross. In the garden he poured out his feelings, frustrations, heartache, fear, and pain. This was where Jesus wrestled with God. He felt "very sorrowful, even to death" (v 38) and brought these extreme emotions to his Father in prayer. Then Jesus modeled to us the sufferer's prayer: *Take away my suffering, but if not, I will bow to your will.* Jesus asked God to take away his cup of suffering, but he was still willing and submissive. Wonderfully, Jesus submitted to the Father's will to drink every last drop of the cup of human suffering and death.

We know that the suffering in our lives doesn't always lift when we want it to. It can stick around for what feels to us like much too long. For some, it lasts for a season; for others, it only lifts when they go home to Jesus. But how we, as mothers, respond to suffering in our lives will impact both our families and our own relationship with the Lord. When suffering comes, we can look to Christ: the one who drank the cup for us.

THE GARDEN OF DEPRESSION: JENNIFER'S STORY

Postpartum depression (PPD) hit Jennifer less than 24 hours after giving birth, though it was a few months later that she was officially diagnosed by her doctor. She says:

The pervasive sadness and rampant worry didn't only affect my ability to bond with my baby; it seemed to drive a wedge between me and the Lord. I couldn't pray beyond a few sporadic requests for him to help me survive the next 24 hours. I knew he was good. I knew he was there. I just couldn't feel any affection toward him or from him.

After struggling with infertility and adopting her first son, she didn't expect that the labor and delivery for her second son would change her so much.

The illusion of control shattered. The fatigue and erratic emotions of PPD wore me out so much, I couldn't juggle all the responsibilities of caring for a newborn and a toddler, let alone make dinner or take a shower.

Jennifer realized she had to ask for help, and the increased dependence crushed her pride. PPD was changing her daily life, but it was also doing valuable work: killing her pride and self-sufficiency.

God showed me that I needed to die to self-sufficiency, and accept the mercy of his provisions and the sustaining power of his presence.

Jennifer never asked God to bring about circumstances that would humble her, but she learned to thank him for them. As she gradually and painfully pried her clenched fingers off from her expectations and plans, the Lord reordered the way she viewed her will versus his will.

I started turning to him more often than I used to,
asking him to work in my kids' lives, to guide them
by his wisdom, and to raise them up to follow him.

Though it didn't happen all at once, the way Jennifer responded to the "death" of suffering in her life paved the way for the "resurrection" that God wanted to work inside her heart.

(While the "baby blues" are quite common, and something that I struggled with myself, PPD is much more serious and may need professional help. If you are worried about yourself or about someone you know, please do something about it right away. A good starting point would be either your pastor, your doctor, or a mental-health professional. Don't struggle on alone. Ask for help.)

THE GARDEN OF CRISIS: NANCY'S STORY

Their child was dying and it only started with strep throat. Twelve-year-old Tina came home from school complaining of a sore throat. It wasn't the first time. So her mom took her to the doctor and got the routine antibiotics. But over the next few weeks Tina's parents began noticing strange symptoms. Their daughter was turning into a different person. They realized she had PANDAS (Pediatric Autoimmune Neuropsychiatric Disorders Associated with Streptococcal Infections). When Tina got strep throat she had an auto-immune response to the sickness that allowed the streptococcal bacteria to cross the blood-brain barrier and enter her brain. In such cases it manifests in the basal ganglia of the brain and causes OCD, anxiety, TICS, mood and personality changes, school regression, and other symptoms.

Tina and her parents had to travel out of state to seek treatment. It was only meant to take three days, but Tina didn't recover. Instead she had a negative reaction to the treatment, which landed her in the ER numerous times, and eventually in hospital for surgery. In the week leading up to the hospital stay, Tina's mom, Nancy, had her "Gethsemane moment".

Our daughter was slowly slipping from our hands. She was dying. The treatments were not working as the doctor had encouraged us they would. I remember lying on the hotel couch one day and praying to God that his will would be done. Whether it was to heal our daughter, take her to heaven, or leave us in prolonged suffering, I wanted to be able to submit to his plan for her life.

I had to mentally give my twelve-year-old daughter's life over to God. I had no control. Nothing in my most powerful mothering abilities of protection could save her. Not even doctors knew what to do. She was truly in God's hands. I let go. I wept. I prayed harder than I knew possible. I shook. Knowing fully that my words were not falling on deaf ears, but on to the lap of the Almighty, I said, "not my will, but yours." In that moment I felt fear, but also deep peace.

What was supposed to be three days turned into three weeks. Eventually Tina stabilized enough to leave hospital, but it wasn't how the family wanted to return home. Tina's life was spared, but she still (as I write this) has recurring symptoms from PANDAS: separation anxiety, OCD, mood and personality changes, major mood swings, school regression, insomnia, migraines, and frequent pain. Tina's parents don't have the daughter they used to have. She isn't the same student anymore either. Nancy says:

I have to die daily to my new normal. I have to stop comparing her to what she used to be and accept that this is still the same child, but different. It is hard to not compare and push. It is hard to accept changes. It is hard for both of us.

Tina was regularly babysitting her siblings. Now, she cannot babysit. We went from feeling as if we had finally "arrived" as parents—because we had a built-in babysitter—to having a child who cannot care for her siblings at all.

I had to give up my new career. I had gone back to school and got my real estate license, because all of my children were finally in school. Now I can't work. She is my full-time job. I had to give up a lot of my hobbies, date nights, trips, and vacations. We simply cannot live as we used to.

Nancy is more than familiar with the "death" of suffering. Though she submitted to God's will back in the crisis stages, she still wrestles with God and has to live with the daily reality of a life that has been turned upside down and might never be the same again. She says:

We never had a miracle, Tina is not healed, but the Lord has shown himself strong and has walked us

through the valley. I have learned the power of the
name of Jesus. It can bring light to the darkest of
situations and cause the atmosphere to change even if
circumstances do not.

One of the biggest lessons Nancy has learned is not to take
the hard moments for granted.

This path God has brought us on is not the wrong
way or a detour. I have learned to stop looking back
to how it used to be … wishing for the past. This is
his perfect path; this is not a mistake. We are right
where he wants us, suffering and all. I have learned
to embrace the hard and lean [on] him more.

Though Nancy has experienced many daily "deaths," and
still does, the Lord has brought "resurrection" in her heart
by showing her that her joy is found only in him: not in her
circumstances, not in her children—in nothing but knowing
him more deeply. She says it has driven her to the feet of
Jesus, and for that she is grateful.

THE GARDEN OF AUTISM: JANELLE'S STORY

Janelle's two boys were diagnosed with autism. Her "Gethsemane moment" came when she took her eldest child (then
three) to a developmental pediatrician. They spent two hours
testing him and confirmed what Janelle had already known:

Yes, he was different, and yes, our story was not
going to be what I had always imagined it would
be. I got home and sobbed. And then I called my

*Mom and told her, "If this is God's will for our
lives, I want it. I don't want to go somewhere he isn't
leading, and if he is leading us down a road I didn't
expect, at least I know with certainty that he is on it
with me." There was such comfort, knowing that not
only were my suspicions true and I wasn't crazy, but
that God had known all along that this is where he
wanted to take me.*

Though Janelle had this amazing moment when God gave
her the grace to accept and submit to his will for her life, she
still wrestles with God's will and his purpose for her children.

*I've come to accept the reality that there is a fine line
between trusting God and struggling to believe that
what he has for me and my kids is good.*

Janelle loves her boys, and finds joy in mothering, while also
experiencing the particular challenges of parenting autistic
children. Raising her children affects every aspect of her daily
life. Daily sensory meltdowns that can last for hours, while
trying to prevent physical injury, are draining. She says the
most challenging aspect is the suffering that comes with not
being able to verbally communicate with her younger son.
She has submitted to this call on her life, while at the same
time acknowledging and accepting the fact that her daily
"walking it out" is deeply tiring. As she puts it:

*I'm not sure how I'm supposed to just be "ok" when
my life feels so unpredictable and as if I'm constantly
getting in a train wreck.*

And yet the many "deaths" Janelle has faced in accepting this call have brought her many "resurrection" lessons. Autism has drawn her heart closer to Christ. She says her "capacity for love has increased a thousandfold" as mothering autistic boys has shown her how much patience and love she needs from God. He has also taught her about how unlimited he is when she is frustrated by her limitations.

> *God can speak to my youngest son's heart, and it probably isn't going to be primarily through my words. God can settle my other son's emotional turmoil, and use that passion to further his kingdom.*

For Janelle, God has "busted out of all the boxes" she placed him in. He is using the "deaths" in her life with autism to bring about the truth of "resurrection" in her heart, even while she still wrestles with the goodness of his will. She knows Jesus wrestled with accepting the Father's will in the garden (Matthew 26 v 38-39), and this is a comfort to her in suffering.

THE GARDEN OF CHRONIC ILLNESS: CHELSEA'S STORY

> *Shortly after my third son was born, I was diagnosed with an extremely rare medical condition called autoimmune progesterone anaphylaxis. In layman's terms, I'm allergic to my own progesterone (the female sex hormone). Anytime my hormone levels rise, I run the risk of having an allergic reaction*

ranging from mild hives to life-threatening anaphylactic shock.

There is no cure, aside from removing my ovaries and uterus, and that's not a viable option as a thirty-something. For now, I'm able to manage my physical symptoms pretty well, but I do still deal with physical discomfort and anxiety each month as my body anticipates another menstrual cycle.

Chelsea lived in perpetual fear before her diagnosis.

I had no idea when I'd experience another attack, and with three small boys at home who weren't yet old enough to call for help, my biggest fear was that something would happen to me when my husband was at work and that the boys would be alone with no one to watch over them. I did everything I could think of to protect them. I bought a medical ID bracelet. I carried an epi-pen and a phone on my person at all times. I had an army of friends and family ready at the helm. But it wasn't enough. I had to put my need for control to death and trust God with my life and the lives of my children, moment by moment.

Chelsea has asked God to heal her, but every time she's prayed that prayer, he has shown her how he's using her illness to bring him glory.

I've had women reach out to me from around the world who have seen my social-media posts about my disease, and I've been able to share the hope of Christ with them. I've been able to better comfort friends who are suffering because I've seen God's faithfulness through my own suffering. I've grown closer to God because I've felt my deep need for him.

Chelsea has had her moments of wrestling with the will of God in her suffering, just as Jesus did in the Garden of Gethsemane. But ultimately, she says, she's made a choice to trust God with her life and the lives of her children, while also admitting her weakness and looking to him for help and strength. God is putting to "death" her need for control through the suffering of chronic illness, and this is producing the fruit of "resurrection" in her own heart and the hearts of other women who suffer.

GOD'S PLAN FOR HUMAN SUFFERING

At one level, these stories about Jennifer, Nancy, Janelle, and Chelsea are unusual. They show extreme levels of struggle and pain. But at another level they are also normal, as every single one of us suffers at one time or another. You may battle with pain—not life-threatening but a daily weight you have to carry. Or maybe you were a successful executive, and now you're "just" a mom and feel your life got very small. God will use these daily struggles, whatever they are, to bring you to your own "garden moments." *Will you submit to his will for your life in these moments?*

No one wants to suffer. Even Jesus didn't naturally desire suffering when he was in anguish in the Garden of Gethsemane. He wrestled with the Father's will, but then wonderfully submitted to it. This submission didn't mean it was easy for him. The same is true for us.

To be human in this world means suffering. It was introduced in another garden, the Garden of Eden, and every person since then has experienced that pain. But the promise we have in Christ is that one day our human suffering will be no more (Revelation 21 v 1-5). Everything in us, and in this world, will be fully restored to perfection. In the meantime, God uses the "deaths" in suffering to bring about spiritual life in us. As we've seen with the four stories above, God has a clear purpose and plan for human suffering, just as he had the best purpose and plan in mind with the suffering of his only Son, Jesus.

Be encouraged by the example of Christ: that, though he did submit to the will of the Father in his suffering, it was still hard for him, and he still wrestled. We can look to Jesus, the Suffering Servant (Isaiah 52 v 13 – 53 v 12), as our hope and our comfort when we suffer. And if we ask him, the Holy Spirit will help us to submit to the work of suffering in our lives too.

FOR YOUR HEART AND LIFE

Write a letter to your future self. Imagine what the fruit of your suffering might be five or ten years from now. Imagine the lessons you might learn, the things you might see and know, the opportunities you might gain through it, and even the heartache that might stay and the questions that will still linger.

Dear Jesus,

Thank you that you submitted to the Father's will for your life and death. Thank you for taking and drinking the cup of suffering for me. Because you suffered, I now have hope that one day my suffering will end. Please comfort me in my suffering with the comfort you received from the Father. I pray that the Holy Spirit would give me the grace to submit to the will of God in my suffering, even though it continues to be hard and I still wrestle with it and question you. Help me to persevere and strengthen me for the road ahead.

In your mighty name, Amen

Journaling Space

CHAPTER 6

Following His Pattern

Sometimes motherhood can just be too much. There are many times when I reach my breaking point, and it feels so hard. At those times the feelings can be overwhelming and the tears recurring. It's complete exhaustion at every level. It's not just the physical needs of my children that are demanding, but their emotional, mental, and spiritual needs as well. I'm playing the peacemaker between my two sons, I'm counseling, I'm working through character development and discussing heart issues. Just a day of working through behavioral issues can be enough to drain me.

And yet I would never trade my life for another. I love what I do and feel privileged to be able to do it. The joy of answered prayers for my children, or witnessing growth and understanding in their lives, can be so rewarding. No wonder moms feel like they are going crazy! We can feel such a range of emotions on any given day. Joy, fear, love, sorrow, pain, fatigue.

It's through this range of emotions that we see a pattern emerge in our lives: a pattern of daily death and resurrection. Because of how hard motherhood can be, it can sometimes feel like a cross to carry. The "death" we feel is a death to ourselves: our independence, parts of our identity, our time, our bodies, and so on. It's a constant laying down of our lives. The hardships inherent in motherhood are like the initial death that a grain of wheat undergoes as it is buried in the earth. But the only way for the life of the harvest to emerge is through the death of that very seed. The life of Jesus was such a "seed," poured out and spent in service and then buried in death (John 12 v 24-26). But at the end of it all there was life: new, glorious, resurrection life. Now we, as mothers, can look to Jesus as our example, in his life, death, and bodily resurrection. We too can be a seed like him.

A LIFE OF SERVICE

We have much to learn from Jesus in the seeming quietness and hiddenness of motherhood. He can sympathize with us because, in entering our world, he took on a hidden role. In the first 30 years of his life, Jesus mostly seemed ordinary. He probably grew up to be a workman, learning the carpentry trade from Joseph. Even during the last three years of his time on earth, although his miracles and teaching drew the crowds, Jesus regularly went away by himself or quietly spent time with just a few disciples.

Much of motherhood encompasses serving without being noticed or appreciated, like the ministry of Jesus himself. He lowered himself by becoming a man, and in a similar smaller way a mother lowers herself to deal with diaper changes and potty time—small things that feel below us. We were once the center of our lives, and then a helpless newborn came along to show us that we are no longer at the center. Jesus humbled himself when he left his home in heaven and became a man living on the fringes of society. He made himself low to lift us up (Philippians 2 v 6-8).

Jesus was constantly serving, healing, and teaching. Rest was elusive. What mother can not relate to that? These similarities between the ministry of Jesus and human ministries like motherhood are what make the serving of others so hard. I've had low feelings about motherhood, when I'm so exhausted that I think, "Why am I throwing my life away like this?" But I have to remind myself that even when motherhood doesn't feel rewarding, it's working something better in me than a life spent in self-seeking.

Living a life in service of others is never a life thrown away. Jesus' life shows this to be true. When life was hard for Jesus, he may have been tempted to think, *Why bother? These stubborn, selfish people aren't worth it.* But thankfully, he never thought that way. His mission was a life of service, lived perfectly for us. This made him the perfect sacrifice in our place. Jesus was exhausted and depleted for our eternal salvation. He can surely give us the grace to carry on when our own ministry is hard.

Jesus' sacrifice looked unimportant and insignificant to humanity, but, veiled to the natural eye there was great glory because his actions reaped eternal benefits for his people (Hebrews 9 v 15). In a similar but far smaller way, your hidden sacrifices as a mother who seeks, in Christ, to live to the glory of God, are not unimportant or insignificant because underneath the nose-wiping, tears, and tantrums is a great glory resulting in eternal benefits.

LIKE JESUS IN HIS DEATH

We tend to think that life precedes death, but in the kingdom of God the reverse is true: death precedes life. It's the pattern Jesus left behind for us. He taught that we must die to self in order to experience any true life in our hearts. As Paul says:

> *... that I may know him and the power of his resurrection, and may share his sufferings, becoming like him in his death.*
>
> *Philippians 3 v 10*

We become like Jesus in his death when we put to death the sin in ourselves and deny ourselves for the sake of others. This is why motherhood is so hard: not just because we are weak and needy but because we are sinful as well. The hard things of motherhood are like sandpaper, rubbing back our rough edges and making us smooth. The Holy Spirit is using motherhood to refine us, whether that's through the death of our expectations in motherhood, as we talked about in chapter 1, or the mundanity of daily motherhood seen in chapter 2.

The disappointment of unexpected circumstances can be a small-scale death for us. It's a type of loss—something that reeks of the curse, which began in Eden. For me, that looked like a ruined birth plan, a hard labor and delivery, a newborn in the NICU, baby blues, and sleepless nights. I didn't expect to feel sadness and loneliness when I brought my baby home.

There is also a feeling of dying to self when we live out the mundanity of daily motherhood. The ordinary small things of motherhood can be like the annoyance of a dripping faucet. Motherhood often means dying to those things in life that seem more exciting or adventurous to us. Embracing the ordinary can feel so hard as we forsake the "bigger things" for now or maybe forever.

The burdens we feel in motherhood can be deathlike in their grip on us. The crushing weight can press on us without relief, as we saw in chapter 3, when I talked about my need to be strong enough. I thought something was wrong with me as a mom if I needed to ask for help. I thought I should be able to do it all myself.

Motherhood can also be fraught with weakness, as we thought about in chapter 4. Weaknesses and failures can feel like a lesser type of death, because they are evidence of brokenness in our lives. Brokenness is part of the curse upon our earth, which began with sin. Weakness is also humbling, so our pride is being put to death.

Suffering in motherhood can feel like death, whether that's through living with chronic illness, dealing with postpartum depression, or walking through crises, as in chapter 5.

When we embrace the daily deaths we face as mothers, we can humbly offer our struggles to God. He will meet us in our depression, anxiety, stress, sleep deprivation, anger, frustration, and lack of patience. This is exactly where he wants us. This humble embracing of death is fertile ground for new and deeper life.

KNOW HIS RESURRECTION

We must become like Jesus in his death in order to know the power of his resurrection through the Holy Spirit. This is true for martyrs being burned at the stake and, in a far smaller way, for new mothers facing sleepless nights. It is true at the end of our lives and throughout our days on earth. We must bury ourselves like a grain of wheat, so that our death will bear fruit (John 12 v 24).

But through the dying, beauty is birthed. God uses the curse of death to bring new life. And it's the only way to the joy of true life. As Paul says:

> *For as by a man came death, by a man has come also the resurrection of the dead. For as in Adam all die, so also in Christ shall all be made alive.*
>
> 1 Corinthians 15 v 21–22

Adam brought death, but Jesus went through death to bring us resurrection (a spiritual resurrection in our souls and a bodily resurrection to come). Because of Jesus, we now have this daily cycle of resurrection in our souls, because "our inner self is being renewed day by day" (2 Corinthians 4 v 16). We are daily renewed—able to persevere in faith despite suffering the deaths of persecution and decay—because we know the power of the resurrection. Jesus shows us that we will never experience resurrection (in our souls and bodily) without embracing death to our sinful ways.

This is how we come to Christ, but it's also how we continually grow and flourish into Christ's likeness until we physically die. Christ came to bring abundant life for us (John 10 v 10), but he purchased that life by tasting death. He calls every one of his children to walk this same road (Mark 8 v 34). He gives us tastes of the abundant life of resurrection when we choose to follow this road.

Changing how we look at our lives as moms helps us to see glimpses of God working in our lives. That's what we've been thinking about in the preceding chapters. When I saw my daily acts of self-denial as those of a mother following in the footsteps of Christ, I felt flickers of "resurrection" hope. When I walked through the death of my expectations as a first-time mom, Christ redeemed those hardships by showing me my need for him (from chapter 1). He "resurrected" (or brought to life through the Spirit) my dependency on him.

When I realized how mundane and ordinary motherhood could be, God "resurrected" my perspective to see the bigger picture of glory that the tiny moments make (chapter 2). And when I wouldn't share the burdens of motherhood, God "resurrected" my soul through teaching me to embrace the humility of rest (chapter 3). I am being shown who I really am in all my failures and weaknesses for my good and his glory (chapter 4). And the specific "death" of suffering can bring "resurrection" in our hearts when we submit to the Father's will (chapter 5).

Dying these daily deaths of motherhood has also been the means by which the Spirit imparts the peaceful fruits of "resurrection" in my heart.

FROM DEATH TO LIFE

Death is a curse that God imposed on our world because of the sin of Adam (Genesis 2 v 17), but God brings good out of the bad—he brings resurrection in all its forms. And a "resurrection" in our heart does not depend on our circumstances changing. It's a work of the Spirit in our hearts giving us peace and joy regardless of our situation. It's a place we come to with Job, a man who lost everything but who still humbly submitted to God's will, when he said:

> *Behold, I am of small account; what shall I answer you? I lay my hand on my mouth.*
>
> *Job 40 v 4*

The type of humility that Job exhibits here is fertile ground for the fruit of new life in our hearts. A humble heart is ripe for the fruit of the Holy Spirit to flourish there.

Though death is part of the curse that God imposed because of the first family's sin (Genesis 3 v 22-24)—and it certainly feels wrong in all its forms—God reshapes death into the gateway to life.

Talking of death sounds so morbid, but what God is really calling us to is *life*; he just desires us to walk through death as a means to that end. As we've seen in previous chapters, Jesus told us:

> *Truly, truly, I say to you, unless a grain of wheat falls into the earth and dies, it remains alone; but if it dies, it bears much fruit.*
>
> *John 12 v 24*

The fruit of Jesus' death has covered the globe and continues to grow wherever the gospel is spread. If we, like the grain of wheat, let ourselves be buried and die, God will grow through us an abundance of fruit for ourselves and others.

I didn't expect "death" when I first became a mother. I was surprised by the dark struggle. Motherhood has humbled me. It has shown me how weak and needy I really am. This is a good death to die, and I die it daily. I die deaths through sleepless nights, nonstop service, countless interruptions, and sacrifice of my time and energy (let alone sacrifice of my body and mental capacity). The way we respond to these daily deaths is crucial for their purpose in our lives. Bitterness and apathy will only make them worse, but humble acceptance and desperate cries to the Holy Spirit for help will turn these deaths into "resurrections".

If we view these deaths as opportunities to draw close to our Father, they are worth it, just for that. Every day I'm reminded of my weakness and my great need for Christ to work in me and my children. But my "resurrection" moment in motherhood came when I saw what God was killing in me: my self-sufficiency. Motherhood has shown me that I'm not strong enough and I'm not good enough. There is nothing in me, in and of myself, that can make me be *enough*.

When we admit that we're weak mothers, we have a fuller realization of how strong a God we serve. This is the place of death, where God swoops down and displays his resurrection power to us through the work of the Holy Spirit, who raised Christ from the dead. In him we are strong enough for all the daily deaths of motherhood, and we can look to him to bring the fruit of new life in our souls.

FOR YOUR HEART AND LIFE

This week consider planting a seed for indoors or outdoors. Think about how the seed is buried and "dies" in the ground. You can't see it anymore. But then observe it and watch as it grows and reminds you of the resurrection of life. If you don't have time for this (or any seeds!), do an online search for a timelapse video of a seed germinating.

Dear Lord,

You are the resurrection and the life (John 11 v 25). You have shown us the way we must walk when we follow you, and that is the path of self-denial. Help me not to fight your process of death and resurrection in my life, but help me to die to self. Give me grace to pour myself out in service to my child. I can't do any of this without the power of the Holy Spirit, and I trust him to give me strength daily as I walk with you.

In your name, Amen

Journaling Space

CHAPTER 7

Resurrected Motherhood

All year round the thorn of the gorse bush has been hardening and sharpening. Even in spring, the thorn does not soften or fall off. But at last, about halfway up, two brown furry balls emerge. They are small at first, but then they fully break out of last year's thorn to flower into a ray of sunshine. The hardness gives way to a delicate beauty. The death of the thorn splits open to produce a blossoming resurrection of life.

This pattern of death and resurrection is in nature, but we've also seen this pattern in motherhood. The daily "deaths" of struggles: the limitations, the failures, the helplessness, the suffering. The thorns. But truly what is offered here is the flower of life. These hardships are the road to joy, because they bring us to our knees before the Father. This doesn't mean motherhood becomes less hard, but it means our perspective has changed. He lifts up our eyes and raises our gaze to new heights.

THE JOY SET BEFORE US

Jesus lived a humble life that we can learn from as mothers. The Bible says that he "set his face" towards Jerusalem (Luke 9 v 51): the place of his trial and execution. That was the end of his ministry, but not the final end, as we know. In all the grueling labor, sacrifice, and service, Jesus was looking to the glory to come when he would rise from the dead and win back his people for eternity.

He lived his whole life, public and private, doing ministry for joy that was to come, even if it wasn't in the moment. Jesus died to himself moment by moment when he served others, and yet he knew his resurrection would bring life for us. He shows us that the ministry of motherhood can be a joy and a privilege, though it is sometimes deathlike in its weariness.

> *Therefore, since we are surrounded by so great a*
> *cloud of witnesses, let us also lay aside every weight,*
> *and sin which clings so closely, and let us run with*
> *endurance the race that is set before us, looking to*
> *Jesus, the founder and perfecter of our faith, who*
> *for the joy that was set before him endured the cross,*
> *despising the shame, and is seated at the right hand*
> *of the throne of God.*
>
> *Hebrews 12 v 1-2*

These verses in Hebrews follow the section about people in the Bible who persevered in the faith amid trials and suffering. They must have been tired and weary, like moms. But they looked ahead to the promise of the Savior: *the joy set before them.* These believers saw with eyes of faith even when they never saw Jesus come in their lifetime. These ones who went before us are our cloud of witnesses cheering us on.

Those who are in our local church families today can cheer us on as well, if we take time to foster these supportive relationships. Don't struggle on by yourself. It's good to let other believers know about your struggles and hardships, and to ask for prayer and support. The church past, but also the church present and local, is meant to cheer us on.

The joy set before Jesus was every Christian. It was us. He looked forward to bringing his children home safely. He knew his death and resurrection would accomplish this. He put our best interest first before his own. What glorious news, that we are so dearly loved!

Today, as moms, the joy set before us is the second coming of our Savior. We see it with eyes of faith even if it won't happen in our lifetime. The joy before us is also eternal rest with Jesus, seeing the fruit of our labors through heavenly eyes. Until then we mother with eyes of faith. We "die" moment by moment, while we serve our children in ways unseen to the rest of the world (or social media), but we can also look to the "resurrection" set before us by fixing our eyes on Jesus.

HARDSHIPS TURNED TO JOY

It's hard to have joy when motherhood feels hard. It's not something we can conjure up on our own. Self-help books and positive talk won't produce it. It's something deep inside our souls that only the Holy Spirit can bring about. But there are things we can do to help make our hearts fertile for the work of the Spirit to produce fruit in us. We can choose to accept the hard things of motherhood as a tool of discipline in our lives. We can be trained by them. Hardships are part of the discipline of the Lord for our good (Hebrews 12 v 5-7). Submitting to the work of the Spirit in our lives in this way will be the way we set our eyes on joy. Why not pause for a moment and ask yourself: *What would it look like this week for me to submit to the work of the Spirit in my life?*

When I faced the hardship of a difficult birth and postpartum baby blues, alongside the stress of caring for a newborn, it threw me on my knees before the Father. Throwing my needy self at him was exactly what I needed. My strength was replaced by his. Striving in my own strength leads to weary defeat, but pleading for his strength leads to my joy.

The ordinary moments of motherhood can feel so mundane and pointless, but if we look at every tiny act, prayer, and word as advancing God's kingdom in our homes, it can bring us joy. Raising up the next generation will only happen in ordinary moments of the day, one after the other. And bringing our burdens to Christ will lead to happiness in him. Carrying the weight of motherhood, all on our own, will lead to our prideful downfall, but humbling ourselves to find our rest in Christ will lead to joy.

The Spirit's work is not just seen in our success and triumphs but in our weakness and failures. Motherhood helps us see who we are in light of who God is. But it's painful to see those things at first: it's painful to see all the dirt when the light comes on in what we thought was a clean room. But seeing the dirt is the first step to getting it clean. This works the same way in our hearts as it does in the rooms of our homes. But when we tackle the mess in our homes, and in our hearts, we'll find the joy that was always set before us.

This joy ahead of us typically comes after experiencing hardship or suffering. Sometimes the promise of joy doesn't come until all of life's hardships and struggles come to an end when we pass into eternity. We know that the joy set before us is ultimately to be fully felt and experienced in heaven, but we can have tastes of it here on earth. Many times those "tastes" come through the "death" of hardship. Jesus wasn't just handed resurrection—he earned it with his sinless life, his suffering, his obedience, and his blood.

We know that joy is a gift that we cannot earn, but we do tend to seek it in superficial ways that don't require much of us. We want good feelings that bypass any pain. But this type of feeling is fleeting. Deep everlasting joy is developed over time from submitting to and embracing hardship, from wrestling with suffering, and from the willingness to sacrifice and be inconvenienced. It's good to remember these truths when motherhood is hard: that if we yield to the spiritual discipline motherhood brings, we'll reap a harvest of fruit. Jesus went this way, and he calls you to follow him (Matthew 16 v 24). When everyone wants the easy and comfortable road, Jesus says to take the difficult one (Matthew 7 v 13-14).

JOY COMES WITH THE MORNING

At the end of Jesus' hard road was the joy of resurrection. A mom's road is often paved with hardship, but by the work of the Holy Spirit, who is using motherhood as our train-ing ground, we can experience "resurrection" joys through changed hearts and minds.

Jesus said:

> *I am the resurrection and the life. Whoever believes*
> *in me, though he die, yet shall he live.*
>
> *John 11 v 25*

He is our hope of eternal life. But while we wait for our lit-eral resurrection, our "resurrection" every day is the hope of Jesus himself. Jesus is the resurrection. When all we feel is the "death" of hardship in motherhood, we can remember that we have Jesus, who is the resurrection. All the "deaths" we've talked about in this book are meant for our good—to drive us to the one who is the resurrection.

We can put false hope in our expectations and plans, in "big" things that don't feel mundane, in our own ability to juggle everything, in our good behavior and "having it all together," and just in our little kingdoms of "self." But those false hopes will eventually fail us. They will die. So, what are you building your hope on? We must build our life founda-tion on a person—Jesus Christ, who is our resurrection. The daily "deaths" of motherhood should bring us to him. He is your only true hope and joy.

> *Sing praises to the LORD, O you his saints,*
> *and give thanks to his holy name.*
> *For his anger is but for a moment,*
> *and his favor is for a lifetime.*

Weeping may tarry for the night,
  but joy comes with the morning.

Psalm 30 v 4-5

With Jesus, our resurrection, we have hope. Like David in Psalm 30, we can have joy in the morning (v 5). But before David tells us about the morning joy, he warns us that "weeping may tarry for the night." And then, a few verses later, he joyfully says:

You have turned for me my mourning into dancing;
  you have loosed my sackcloth
  and clothed me with gladness.

Psalm 30 v 11

God can give us the sweet relief of a new day. Much as when a mother gets to "turn off" (sometimes) at the end of a long day and find some relief in time spent alone or with her husband. The morning (especially after a previous day filled with tantrums, spit-up, and bad attitudes) signifies relief, hope, and light coming into darkness. David is telling us that there is another side. Jesus will bring us through the darkness of struggle and hardship.

We know this will finally and fully happen when he makes a new heaven and a new earth (Revelation 21 v 1), and when the joy of seeing Jesus face to face brings total healing and rest. But until that day he promises to strengthen us with his presence right now and every day (Matthew 28 v 20).

The Lord can turn our mourning into dancing in this life by turning our hard circumstances around for our good. His

Spirit can give us peace and joy when we ask and when we desperately need it. His joy alone will carry us through.

FOR YOUR HEART AND LIFE

Find a song that reminds you of the hope and joy of a new morning. Play that song every morning this week.

Dear Jesus,

Thank you for making me your joy. Thank you that you died and rose again for me. Help me, by the Spirit's power, to keep my eyes on you and make you the joy of my life. Help me to put my hope in you and not in false hopes that will let me down. You are truly the resurrection and the life.

Amen

Journaling Space

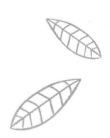

Conclusion:
Looking back

When you come to the end of a road, it's good to look back and see where you've been: to see what you've learned along the way and remember the progress you've made. When the Israelites crossed over the Jordan river and into the promised land, they were commanded by God to set up memorial monuments (Joshua 4 v 1-7). These stones, which were set up where they camped that first night, were used as reminders of where they had been and what God had done for them. They were also intended to provide teaching moments for their children, so that each generation would be reminded of God's goodness.

As you have come to the end of this book, it's good to take a look back and see how God has worked in you and what he's shown you. This gives us hope for the future.

Perhaps you entered motherhood with certain expectations, but you were disappointed with the reality. I know I did and was. I look back and remember how God showed me my weakness and vulnerability as a new mom. My lack of control was deeply felt.

As we saw in chapter 2, God does extraordinary things through ordinary means. So much of motherhood is made up of tiny moments that can feel insignificant. Though there might be hardships of "death" in the everyday moments, they are sowing a bigger picture of life.

Looking back we also see that finding rest as moms means coming to the end of ourselves to rely on the one who carries our burdens. When you humbly die to your self-sufficiency, you can find the "resurrection" power you need in him. The death of my self-sufficiency has been a big one in motherhood. I'm continually reminded of my limitations and trying to live inside of them, while I trust God with my family.

Our weaknesses and failures have a purpose for God's glory and our own good. But there is a hardship in realizing we are fallen and flawed. We are "dying" to the view we had of ourselves, while being raised up in our view of God. I know I have had to use my imperfections as a means to humble myself before my children. When I tell them and show them that I don't have it all together, it has an impact on them, because they are seeing that they don't have to live up to a standard of perfection in our home. And then I've been able to point my children to the one who gloriously lived up to that standard of perfection for us.

And when you are called to suffer as a mom, and "go to the garden" as Jesus did, how can you submit to his will while still wrestling with his plan and purpose? Jesus walked the road to Calvary, but he saw joy before him. He shows us the way and feels our pain.

All along the way we've seen motherhood as a pattern of daily death and resurrection. Because of how hard motherhood can be, it feels like a cross to carry. The death you are feeling is a death to yourself: your independence, parts of your identity, your time, your body, and so on. The hardships inherent in motherhood are like the initial death that a grain of wheat undergoes as it is buried in the earth. But the only way for the life of the harvest to emerge is for that very seed to die. Jesus was such a seed and now by his strength, and the power of the Holy Spirit, we can be a seed, like Jesus, every day as moms.

The road of motherhood is paved with mile markers, but we must be intentional about raising up stone memorials in our hearts when we get to those markers. Lean on God, seek him, and see what he might be teaching you through the many "deaths" in motherhood. When he is the "joy set before us," then all the "deaths" are colored with his glory and light. Just when we come to the end of ourselves (yet again), he is there offering us a new beginning. He is the resurrection. And he is all we need to carry on in all the joys and sorrows that come with being a mom.

Books, Magazines, and Websites Referenced

April Brover, *Common Place Quarterly*, Volume 1: Issue 3

G.K. Chesterton, *Orthodoxy* (Moody Publishers, 2009)

Gyo Fujikawa, *A Child's Book of Poems* (Sterling Children's Books, 2007)

Vaneetha Rendall Risner, https://www.crosswalk.com/faith/spiritual-life/how-to-follow-jesus-example-of-rest.html

Jen Wilkin, *None Like Him* (Crossway, 2016)

Acknowledgments

This first book of mine was born out of a dream and a calling from a young age. So, I want to acknowledge my heavenly Father for placing this gift in my life, helping it grow, and making a way for me to write for a wider audience. This is from you and for you.

Next to my God and Savior, my parents' faithfulness in my life has helped bear the fruit of this book. Thank you for always cheering me on and encouraging me in my writing. I know you always knew, Mom.

I would never have written this book without the inspiration of my children. My start with you was rough, Simon, but you showed me how much I love being a mama. I'll always cherish the time I had with just you, before God gave us your brother and sister. Eli and Chloe, you have brought even more joy into our family with both of your arrivals.

Josh, you are the love of my life and my best friend. Thank you for helping make this dream a reality and for always sticking by my side and being so proud of me.

To my agent, Brett Harris, thank you for seeing "something" in my writing and taking the time to reach out and help. It was a long road, but thank you for not giving up and for all the guidance. And to my faithful editor, Alison Mitchell, thank you for helping me. I loved working with you.

Thank you also to all the ladies who helped out with interviews for the chapter on moms who suffer: Janelle, Chelsea, Jennifer, and Nancy. Your stories will help so many moms. Also, to all the people on my email base of supporters (you know who you are). Thank you for all the emails and prayers over the last few years.

Lastly, when I first started "getting my writing out there" and wrote frequently for Desiring God, Tony Reinke was a constant source of encouragement and confirmation when it came to my writing. Thank you for strengthening me as a writer, Tony, and confirming the calling on my life.

Meditations on the Psalms

These meditations on the Psalms look at the emotions we all experience, and how to bring them before God. This inspiring book gives women a language in which to cry out to God in order to help them process their feelings, as well as helping them to grow in their faith.

thegoodbook.com/teach-me-to-feel

30 meditations for women

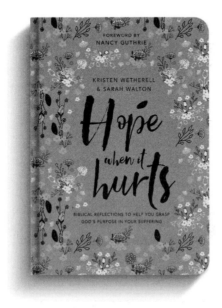

Thirty biblical reflections that are realistic about the hurts of life, yet overwhelmingly full of hope about the God who gives life. A great encouragement to women who are suffering.

thegoodbook.com/hope-when-it-hurts

thegoodbook
COMPANY

BIBLICAL | RELEVANT | ACCESSIBLE

At The Good Book Company, we are dedicated to helping Christians and local churches grow. We believe that God's growth process always starts with hearing clearly what he has said to us through his timeless word—the Bible.

Ever since we opened our doors in 1991, we have been striving to produce Bible-based resources that bring glory to God. We have grown to become an international provider of user-friendly resources to the Christian community, with believers of all backgrounds and denominations using our books, Bible studies, devotionals, evangelistic resources, and DVD-based courses.

We want to equip ordinary Christians to live for Christ day by day, and churches to grow in their knowledge of God, their love for one another, and the effectiveness of their outreach.

Call us for a discussion of your needs or visit one of our local websites for more information on the resources and services we provide.

Your friends at The Good Book Company

thegoodbook.com | thegoodbook.co.uk
thegoodbook.com.au | thegoodbook.co.nz
thegoodbook.co.in